BY THE
STARS

BY THE
STARS

Written by
Jill Wintersteen of Spirit Daughter

SPIRIT DAUGHTER PUBLISHING

Copyright © 2022 by Jill Wintersteen AKA Spirit Daughter

All rights reserved.

No part of this book may be reproduced or used in any manner without written permission of the copyright owner except for the use of quotations in a book review.

For more information contact:
hello@spiritdaughter.com

First paperback edition August 2022

Book design by Rebecca Reitz
Cover design by Rebecca Reitz

ISBN 978-1-954337-81-7 (paperback)

www.spiritdaughter.com

This book is for the cosmic wanderer,
the wave rider, and the moon lover.

It is written from an intuitive connection to the Universe,
a portal for information from the soul to the world.

Its intention is to connect you to your greatness
and oneness with the Universe.

You are everything, and everything is you.

Let the words in this book remind you of that single truth.

Hold space for the unfolding of your wisdom.
It is within you like a seed just waiting to be watered.

Allow these messages to water it.

. . . .

Introduction	pg. 8
Aries	pg. 12
Leo	pg. 26
Sagittarius	pg. 40
Taurus	pg. 56
Virgo	pg. 70
Capricorn	pg. 84
Gemini	pg. 100
Libra	pg. 114
Aquarius	pg. 128
Cancer	pg. 144
Scorpio	pg. 158
Pisces	pg. 172
The Moon	pg. 188

INTRODUCTION

This book is a collection of quotes written to inspire you, bring hope, and tune you into the cosmic frequency. Each quote carries its own message, vibration, and resonance. Each will feel different to you depending on when you read them and what energy you embody when you encounter them. The quotes may take on completely different meanings depending on which version of yourself reads them. These quotes are like any form of art- they are up to you to interpret. Your interpretation will change from day to day and year to year. No interpretation is either right or wrong.

This book is divided into thirteen sections corresponding to the zodiac signs, with one section devoted to quotes about the Moon. Each of the zodiac sign sections begins with an astrological poem that embodies the soul of the sign. Please note the pronoun "she" is used in these poems for aesthetic and artistic purposes. The zodiac signs themselves represent all vibrations, including all genders and non-binary energies.

You may use this book however you wish, but the recommended practice is to start with quiet meditation, then randomly open to the page calling to you. There is no right or wrong way to use this book. You can choose to pick only from quotes corresponding to a particular zodiac sign or from the entire book. For example, only choosing randomly from the Leo quotes when the Moon or Sun is in Leo. You can also focus on the Moon section if you only want inspiration from that energy.

You can also read through a few quotes and decide which one resonates the most with you on a certain day. However you use the book is a personal choice and should resonate with your intuition. When you have chosen a page, take in the message, much like you would if you had just pulled an affirmation card. Meditate on the message and its corresponding zodiac energy.

Consider the quote you pick to be a message from the Universe, a message from your higher self. What is it telling you? What energy is speaking to you? You can even ask the book question and flip to a page for the answer in the form of a quote. Sit with the quote for a while and hold it with you throughout your day. Allow it to sink into your consciousness and shift your perception. Allow it to connect you with the Universal wisdom you hold within your energetic field. Allow it to connect you with yourself.

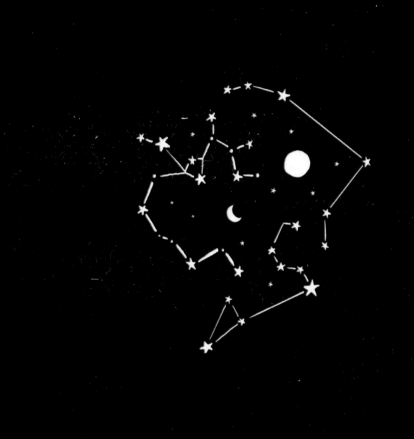

FIRE

ARIES

TRAIL BLAZER. ENTHUSIASTIC. SELF-RELIANT. OPTIMISTIC.

she has a warrior spirit
that is here to develop courage

she approaches life with a
smile and open heart

pressure is her friend and
new experiences fuel her soul

she uses her fire to propel her forward on
a path she does not know, always eager to
find out what the world has to offer her.

the life you want will ask you
to take risks
to be bold
to believe

don't let it down.

instead of being burnt by the fire,

let it fuel you.

believe it is possible and
the Universe will make it possible.

own your power and
get ready to use it.

create a life around what
inspires you the most.

you're about to enter a
new season where you'll be
unstoppable.

even if there are 99 reasons it can't work

find the one reason it will.

allow the road ahead of you to speak louder than the one behind you.

make yourself a priority

even when it makes you feel uncomfortable, or causes you to say no

put yourself first because that's the relationship that matters the most.

she lived a life full of answers
for the questions she dared to ask.

every choice you make
moves you further on your path,

                      even the ones that
                         don't work out.

LEO

COURAGE. WHOLE-HEARTED LIVING. VULNERABILITY. JOY.

fierce with an open heart,
she shines like the sun,
attracting all to her warmth

she is the queen of her world,
walking through fires with her
head held high

close to her flame,
she sets the stage for the impossible,
enjoying every step of the way.

it's time
to step into the vibration
you deserve.

pause,

look back at how far you've come
then look forward and keep going.

your life is about to change
in every direction you want.

unapologetically grow into what you love.

be vulnerable enough to show up,

to face it all with an open heart
and smile that knows

you can rise above it all.

she's the kind of Queen
that walks through fires
with her head held high,

knowing it will all make her
shine even brighter.

it's time to stop playing small
and remember that you are

the stars,
the moon,

and the whole damn universe.

become the leader you've been looking for.

as she stepped through
the fires of her mind,

she knew the flames could never
be hot enough to burn her spirit.

give yourself permission to evolve

past your assumptions
beyond other people's expectations
with confidence and brilliance

into the next version of you.

the magic's at your core

hunt it down

underneath everything you are not
far below the "should's" and "supposed to's"

deep beneath the surface of your soul
you'll find yourself

and she'll feel like home.

SAGITTARIUS

BOLD. EXPANSIVE. SPONTANEOUS. LIVELY.

she was a whirlwind of magic and
courage never attempting to tame her
wild heart as she welcomed adventure
with every bone in her body, leaving
the predictable for the unfamiliar
grounds of the extraordinary

faith was her only vehicle and
she rode it all the way to the
unimaginable.

BY THE STARS

when you believe
the best will happen,

it does.

ingredients for living your dreams:

trust the cycles of life,
be willing to step into the unknown,
embrace the different forms of change,
believe it's all possible,

because it is.

embrace adventures
aligned with your magic.

there are no coincidences
only signs.

trust the magic.

even if you stumble,
you are still learning.

and just when she thought
she was finished,

she expanded,
transformed,

and began again.

manifest with precision,
but don't forget to leave space for
the unimaginable.

sometimes things don't work out as planned,

they work out better.

let go of your old stories,

so the universe can write you new ones.

always look for the magic

which makes the ordinary extraordinary.

buy the plane ticket
quit the job
accept the date
start the company
write the book
sign up for the class
make the call
plan the trip
wander into the unknown
open your heart

take the leap.

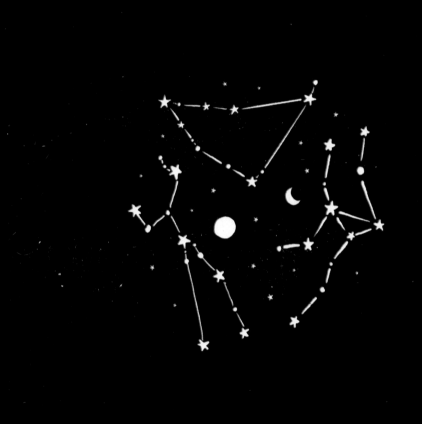

EARTH

TAURUS

CREATIVITY. STILLNESS. BEAUTY. GROUNDING.

BY THE STARS

she knew the key to life was
to rely on herself
which she did in the simplest of ways

a smile under the sunset,
a fresh sheet on her bed
or a sniff of a blooming flower
was all it took to bring her home

she was a Goddess of the Earth
creating magic from her fingertips and
understanding the brilliance of her being
without waiting for anyone to tell her
she was magnificent.

once she surrendered
to the beauty of her life,

all of her fear fell away.

you are the answer you've been looking for.

she stood in awe of nature
as nature stood in awe of her.

in order to stand on the Moon,

she had to feel her feet on the ground.

once she became comfortable
with being uncomfortable,

                        she was free to grow.

abundance is waiting for you.

breathe deep,

you are worthy
of the ground you stand on.

you are your greatest investment.

be patient with yourself,
you are the magic of the Universe

unfolding at its own rhythm.

the path that scares you the most,

is the one you need to take.

dear Universe,

i am ready for more ease,
more abundance,
and more magic.

thank you.

VIRGO

DISCERNMENT. PATIENCE. KINDHEARTEDNESS. SERVICE.

she is made of the same energy as
nature and is just as strong

she stands tall through all of life's
battles knowing that they are no
match for her power

she's as perfect as a field of
wildflowers who dance in the sun
never questioning their brilliance only
embracing their gift to make the
world a more beautiful place.

you can ask for forgiveness,
you can ask for permission,

or you can simply say 'fuck it,'
and do what you want.

a true goddess can never be broken,

wounded - yes,
but broken
never.

she was a walking goddess,
using chaos as a stepping stone
all while reminding the world
of their magic.

it's time to own your truth,

own your power,

and own who the fuck you are.

know your worth
don't ask for it,

state it.

there is no need for a path
when your intuition is guiding you.

you can't stop the Sun from rising,
the Moon from setting, or a
woman who knows what she wants.

goddess move:

signing off for the day
and taking care of yourself.

honor your inner goddess

her visions of magic
that lead your heart
to places unseen.

nurture her energy
hold it close to you
as you feel it heal your soul
and bring light to the world.

trust your intuition
as it speaks of the cosmos
unveiling codes of light
buried in the stars
guiding the way home.

unapologetically step into your power.

make decisions
that reflect your worth, not your fears.

BY THE STARS

CAPRICORN

DILIGENT. WISE. DEVOTED. COMPOSED.

BY THE STARS

she found magic in solitude,
a place to rest her wild heart
and allow the chaos of her soul
to feel at ease

and after she found her center
she began again on a path that
was only hers to walk

never backing down from
an upward climb

she remained determined to reach the
top of her mountain.

you're rare

it's not that you don't fit the world
the world doesn't fit you

but it needs you

your strength
your stories
your wounded lessons

invite the possibility of your life in
shine your beauty
and your magic.

decide how you want to feel

then create a world that supports it.

be willing to say no

so you can hear your yes.

and just like that,
she emerged from the darkness
to greet the day in all her
grace and beauty.

the power to build your dreams has always been in your own two hands.

BY THE STARS

she let go of things
not meant for her
to make room for what could
never miss her.

whether it's

a soft no
a hell no
or even a fuck no

if it's not a resounding yes
it's definitely a no.

you are responsible
for learning the problem

so you can be the solution.

if your dreams don't scare you,

maybe they aren't big enough.

all that matters

is that you believe in yourself.

you can align your whole life
with that kind of energy.

you're the only one
who understands your magic

make time
to get to know it better.

she floats through the world
like wings on a butterfly

using inspiration and magic
to live a life full of answers
to questions she dares to ask

always ready for change
she's the perfect mixture of
curiosity and wisdom.

let go

so the Universe
knows you're ready for more.

uncertainty can bring

fear and doubt
or magic and endless possibilities

it's your choice.

be curious about who you are becoming.

the world needs your knowledge

offer it.

speak your intentions to the Universe

and know you are speaking them into reality.

what you're speaking
you're manifesting

what you're thinking
you're manifesting

what you're believing
you're manifesting

and what you're dreaming
you're manifesting.

change the way you speak to yourself

and change your world.

break free
of your comfort zones
and embrace your potential.

there are parts of yourself
still left to meet.

get ready.

up level your life so much,

you have to re-introduce yourself
to the world.

give yourself credit for

all the times your instinct was right
when you had the courage to ask "why"
when you told the hard truth to someone
when you received the hard truth from someone

and every time you chose love over fear.

believe more in the story of your
future than the story of your past.

she creates balance wherever she
lands, always reflecting the beauty
of the world around her

she needs no one but is happy
to share her life with someone who
appreciates her need for peace

she fills her soul
with everything good in life while
making sure others have the same

she's the one you want on your side
to remind that there are no sides, only
whole experiences of a complex world.

once you learn to calm your internal seas,

no wave can ever throw you off balance.

align with partners who

honor your vibration
raise your vibration
and hold space for your vibration

release ones that lower it.

like the Moon,

stand alone in your greatness
while recognizing the people
who give you light.

put the relationship with yourself first

so you don't become second in your relationships with other people.

even at her best,
she wasn't perfect,

so she surrounded herself
with people who made her better.

you don't have to know the ending
to find peace within the journey.

it's the open, vulnerable,
slightly awkward conversations
that elevate a relationship.

if they're not
raising your vibration,

                          they're lowering it.

we are all made of the same
stars, sun, and moon.

spend time with people
who connect you to the
best version of yourself.

it's ok if you let someone take
your power

just be sure to get it back.

BY THE STARS

she lives in a world
of her own imagination,
where reality is what she makes it
and the only thing holding her
back is herself

fueled by stardust
and a vision of the future,
she leaves a trail of magic as she
dances to her own rhythm

never stopping to conform
to anyone's expectations
but her own.

once she surrendered to who she really was,
all of her fear fell away.

her vision was
magnificent, chaotic,
and misunderstood,
some would even call it mad,
but it led the way to a future
no one else could see.

everything changes when you stop
absorbing the frequency around you

and start defining it.

you have the power to
control the energy of

your space
your body
your heart
and your life

it doesn't control you.

i am attracting:

love
abundance
grace
humility
gratitude

believe it is possible

and the Universe will make it possible.

your dreams manifest
at the speed you believe they will.

it's going to be

bigger than you imagined
happen more quickly than you can believe
and will occur at the exact time you need it.

she had just enough madness
to turn magic into reality.

the hardest step she ever took
was to blindly trust who she was.

you have the power
to shift the frequency
of any space you enter

just by being you.

WATER

CANCER

INTUITIVE. PROTECTIVE. CARING. COMPASSIONATE.

BY THE STARS

she's as delicate as a flower
but strong as the eye of a hurricane.

she follows her intuition
with confidence and conviction as she
travels the emotional waves of her life

never backing down from any storm
that promises to bring her home,
she rises with grace and power
above them all

she's a child of the Moon, and when
her heart is free, she dances under its
light with a smile that lights up
even the darkest night.

forgive yourself for

staying too long
saying the wrong thing
holding onto the past
not allowing yourself to grow
not knowing all the answers
letting an opportunity pass
judging yourself
following old patterns

being human.

from the chaos of her heart

flowed the power of her intuition.

loving yourself is the medicine.

love yourself when you fuck up,
when you make mistakes or
when you talk too much.

love yourself when you lose your way,
when you react to things
that don't deserve your attention,
or you forget your intentions.

love your shadows, your wounds,
and especially the things
you don't want to see.

love all of it.

lessons from the ocean:

go with the flow
but crash when you need to
be beautiful on the surface
but have depths far below
touch as many foreign lands as possible
but belong to none
sparkle all day
but be reflective at night
be soft

but unstoppable.

never apologize for making waves,

even the ocean crashes
so the Earth knows it cannot contain her.

BY THE STARS

learn from the Sun to rise brilliantly

from the Moon to be soft yet strong

and from the Ocean to take up
the space you need.

like the Ocean,

somedays you'll move
slowly and softly
while other days
you'll feel the need
to roar and crash.

both are beautiful.

honor each phase
of your becoming
and unbecoming

                        like the moon,
you shine through all of them.

energies become heavier
right before they release.

it's easier to let go of
what's hard to hold.

fuck up and love yourself anyway.

BY THE STARS

she was half magic, half madness,
the exact meeting of strong and soft,
imperfect but unstoppable

she was the eternal phoenix
rising from the fires she started with
her own two hands

and she never backed down from a
storm that promised to carry
her home.

it's time to unbecome
everything that isn't you.

she who feels everything

has the opportunity to be everything.

you are a constant work in progress,

but also complete as-is.

through the journey

of unraveling,
unbecoming
and unlearning

she found herself.

and like the Moon,
she had a dark side

that not even the Sun could see.

her unbecoming was magical.

she stripped away every layer
the world had placed upon her,
until finally, she found herself.

honor the space between your

old self
                and your
                                new self,

she may feel uncomfortable,
but she's transforming.

and like the Moon,

she had scars from another life but she still shined her brightest in this one.

growth isn't always pretty,

it's necessary.

she transformed her life the way
a snake shed its skin.

slow.
steady.

unafraid of what the world
would think of the mess.

and with no going back.

every fire she went through
became her power,

every wound became
her strength

and every question became
her answer.

BY THE STARS

a perfect blend of stardust and magic,
she danced through the world like every
path was meant for her to walk it

an eternal student of the Universe
she opened herself to the wonders of
the cosmos
always allowing them to
expand her
shape her
and open her heart
to help heal the world

her intuition was never wrong
and when she followed it
the stars rejoiced, the oceans sang,
and the Moon cried in support

she was everything and
everything was her.

you are always connected to

the Ocean's strength
the Sun's brilliance
the Moon's magic

and pure love.

life's not meant to be controlled

it's meant to be lived.

learn from the Moon

to let go in waves
until the next
version of you
slowly appears.

in dreaming

we plant the seeds of our future
we write pages of our life yet to be read
we allow ourselves to speak without fear
we unlock the gates of our heart

we find freedom.

just like the ocean

you are full of untamed magic,

waiting to rise to the surface.

life hack:

if you believe in magic
you're more likely to see it.

wander into the unknown

past your limitations
through your comfort zones
until everything dissolves

then watch as the spaces begin to settle
and your true self emerges

from the nothingness that is
everything.

trust that everything will fall into place without you forcing it there.

never underestimate
the healing power of

the Moon,
the ocean,
or a woman.

a woman shows strength through
softness, magic through the mundane,
and power when it's least expected.

let things fucking end.

BY THE STARS

BY THE MOON

just like the Moon,
you have to trust that each
phase of your life will be more
beautiful than the last.

like the Moon,
you're worthy of appreciation
no matter what phase you're in.

like the Moon, you don't need
to be full to be magnificent.

be like the Moon
and find just as much beauty
in letting go as you do building to full.

like the Moon,
sometimes you need to hide
in order to reset your light.

like the Moon,
let each phase teach you
the beauty of change.

even the Moon has a dark side that
makes her brilliant.

like the Moon,
you can be patient in times of chaos.

just like the Moon,
your imperfections make you
even more beautiful.

like the Moon,
shine the same
no matter if the sky
is full of stars or clouds.

like the Moon,
you too are moving into
the next phase.

like the Moon,
your magic will come
when you least expect it.

like the Moon,
you are on a journey
of highs and lows
darkness and light
new and full

all to end up where you belong.

like the Moon,
you may never be perfect
you'll be something better.

like the Moon,
you too gently influence those
around you without even trying.

like the Moon,
you can always break through
the darkness to find the light.

just like the Moon,
you've been full along.

like the Moon,
your power is always there
even if you appear invisible.

BY THE STARS

like the Moon,
you too can stay steady
even amongst waves of change.

be like the Moon,
shine bright when it's your time
but know when to share the night
with the stars.

and like the Moon,
let your light grow until the world has
no choice but to recognize its power.

BY THE STARS

learn from the Moon
to shine your brightest
no matter what phase you're in.

never be afraid to protect your energy,
there's a reason you don't see
the Moon out every night.

you, like the Moon,
are on your way to full.

be like the Moon,
and learn to let go
while remaining whole.

just like the Moon,
let the things that try to destroy you
make you more beautiful.

🌑

honor each phase
of your becoming

and unbecoming

like the Moon,
you shine through all of them.

learn from the Moon
to stay true to your own rhythm
no matter how much you're misunderstood.

like the Moon,
you'll be a different version tomorrow.

BY THE STARS

ABOUT THE AUTHOR

Jill Wintersteen is a spiritual teacher and the founder of Spirit Daughter, a popular astrology and wellness brand. Through practical, down-to-earth approaches, she uses the framework of astrology to explain topics such as manifestation, energetic evolution, emotional growth, confidence, and self-worth to her many followers. Jill became interested in spirituality as a teenager when she began to pursue studies in astrology, psychology, Chinese Medicine, Yoga, and Meditation. These practices served as the foundation of her life for over twenty years, even as Jill became an academic researcher with a Master's Degree in Psychology. She created an extensive toolkit for herself to help navigate life's unpredictable waters and has made it her life's mission to give those tools to others. Through each of her carefully designed products, Jill gives guidance on the steps needed to manifest one's highest visions. To reach even more people, Jill shares inspirational messages to her community of almost two million followers on Instagram through @spiritdaughter.

Jill is based in Los Angeles, California, where she lives with her two sons, husband, and collie dog.

---

instagram: @spiritdaughter
website: spiritdaughter.com

photo of Jill by: Kathryn Page

✦

always remember,
you are magic.